THE SEASHORE

Martyn Bramwell

Illustrated by Josephine Martin

Kingfisher Books

Contents

Introduction	3
Exploring the Seashore	4
A Very Tough Place to Live	7
The Seashore Naturalist	9

IDENTIFICATION SECTION

Sea Cliffs	10
Rock and Shingle Shores	14
Seaweeds	18
Rock Pools	24
Sandy Shorelines	34
The Seashore Burrowers	38
Exploring the Strand Line	44
The Ever-changing Shoreline	47
Index	48

Kingfisher Books, Grisewood & Dempsey Ltd,
Elsley House, 24–30 Great Titchfield Street,
London W1P 7AD

This edition published in 1990 by Kingfisher Books.
First published in 1986 in paperback by Pan Books Ltd
in the *Piccolo Spotters* series, and in hardback by
Kingfisher Books in the *Fun to Spot* series.
© Grisewood & Dempsey Ltd, 1986

All rights reserved

BRITISH LIBRARY CATALOGUING IN PUBLICATION DATA
Bramwell, Martyn
  Seashore.
  1. Seashore – Juvenile literature
  I. Title II. Martin, Josephine
    910'.09146   GB451.2
ISBN 0 86272 595 X

Phototypeset by Waveney Typesetters, Norwich
Printed in Portugal

Introduction

The coastline is one of the most rewarding **habitats** of all for an amateur nature spotter. The shoreline itself is enormously varied – especially around the edges of Europe and the British Isles. In just a few kilometres you can go from towering cliffs and jagged rocks to long sweeping beaches of sand or **shingle** and then on to the mud-flats of a river **estuary**. Each is a world of its own, with its own special plants and animals.

As soon as you arrive, the questions start. What are those conical holes in the sand at low tide? Why are there different seaweeds on different parts of the beach? What are the puffins and gannets feeding on? Why does the flounder have both eyes on the same side of its head? Who is hunting who in the rock pools?

This little pocket book cannot answer every question. But it can start you off on the right track by showing you a little of what makes coastal habitats tick, what sort of animals and plants you can expect to find there, and how special equipment and behaviour enables them to cope with some of the toughest conditions on earth.

Coastlines can be tough on people too, especially on the careless or foolhardy. If you are going to spend a day exploring the pools and crevices of a rocky shore, spare a thought for your feet. Wear an old pair of gym shoes or trainers to protect them from sharp rocks, and the limpets, mussels and other shells encrusted all over them. You will spend a lot of your time crouching over the pools, so if the sun is hot, wear a shirt and possibly a sun hat too, to avoid getting sunburn. Above all, follow the safety rules and the conservation code on pages 9 and 47: that way you will be safe on the beach – and the beach will be safer for you, for other people coming along later, and for the fascinating variety of plant and animal life that lives there.

Exploring the Seashore

Before taking a closer look at the animal and plant life of the seashore, have a good look at the coastline itself. What shape is it? What is it made of? What forces are wearing it away or building it up? The type of coast depends partly on the type of rock, whether it is hard or soft, lying in horizontal beds or tilted and folded by earth movements in the past, and partly on how strongly the sea is attacking it. Coasts exposed to the full force of the ocean may change quite quickly, while more sheltered coasts can remain almost unchanged for hundreds of years.

Where the sea is pounding away at cliffs of sandstone, limestone or chalk, look out for caves (but do not be tempted inside as many are dangerous). The caves are formed by the force of the water, and the sand and pebbles thrown at the cliff by storm waves, and also by the air that is compressed into cracks in the rock every

Wooden groynes stop sand being swept too far along the beach

Cave and sea stack in a limestone cliff

Deep bay enclosed by headlands of harder rock

time a wave crashes against it. Sometimes a cave will be worn right through a headland to form an arch, but eventually the arch will collapse to leave a sea stack – a favourite nesting place for many seabirds.

Hard rocks resist the action of the sea and often jut out as prominent headlands surrounded by steep cliffs. Softer rocks are more likely to be worn back into bays, with low, gently sloping cliffs or dunes behind them. Beaches of sand and shingle hold other clues. Look carefully at the sand grains and pebbles. Do they come from local rocks? On some beaches you will find pebbles that have come from many kilometres away. If you watch the waves from a high point – a cliff or a high sea wall – you can see that waves hitting the beach at an angle wash up the slope at the same angle then run straight back down the slope. Sand grains and pebbles get carried along this zig-zag path, travelling farther and farther along the coast until the currents and waves are too weak to move them any more and they are dumped on the seabed as sand bars and gravel banks.

Long shingle spit built up by current along the coast

Gently sloping sand dunes backing a sandy beach

GLOSSARY
Algae (plural) Primitive group of plants that includes seaweeds and the green slime on ponds.
Antenna Sense organ on the head of an insect or crustacean.
Aquarium Special tank for keeping fish and other water creatures.
Carapace The hard shell of a crab.
Cast Earth or sand pushed onto the surface from a burrow.
Colony Place where huge numbers of seabirds nest together.
Crustaceans The crab–lobster–shrimp family of animals.
Dorsal On the back.
Estuary The wide mouth of a river where it meets the sea.
Habitat The natural living place of a plant or animal.
Herb Soft-stemmed plant that wilts after flowering.
High Water The highest point reached by the tide.
Larva The grub stage of insect.
Marine Living in the sea.
Mollusc The limpet–cockle–snail–octopus family of animals.
Perennial A plant that flowers year after year.
Plankton Small drifting plants and animals in the sea.
Predator An animal that lives by hunting others.
Prey The victim of a predator.
Scavenger Animal that lives on the dead remains of other animals or on scraps left by others.
Shingle Small rounded pebbles.
Valve Scientists' name for each side of a two-piece shell.

A Very Tough Place to Live

It is difficult to think of the seaside as a particularly tough habitat for animals and plants. But let us take a closer look. Not many years ago, storm waves hurled a 65-tonne concrete block more than 18 metres up a beach in France. Yet the next day most of the seaweed on the shoreline rocks was still there. Seaweeds survive by attaching themselves with exceptionally strong anchors, and instead of resisting the waves they 'give' – swirling and swaying with the water movements. Mussels attach themselves with dozens of strong threads, barnacles glue themselves to the rocks, and limpets clamp themselves in place with a muscular foot.

The plants that grow on cliffs also have to adapt. Most of them grow in dense low cushions to avoid being knocked over by the wind, or send their runners out along the ground. Those that grow low down must cope with constant wetting by salt spray, and with permanently salty soil. And because cliffs are so steep, the plants must rely on tough woody roots to force their way into tiny cracks to obtain a hold.

Perhaps the toughest place of all is the stretch of beach between **high water** and low water. Animals living here have to cope with two completely different worlds. For half the day they are covered with water and must breathe, feed and reproduce underwater. But for the other half of the day they are stranded high and dry – in danger from hunting seabirds and the deadly drying effect of the sun and wind. Here, nature is at her most inventive. Some animals keep cool and damp beneath thick mats of seaweed. Others dig down into the wet sand until the sea returns, while limpets, barnacles and some tube-worms trap water inside their shells to keep them damp while the tide is out.

Just as on land, there are grazers and hunters. When the tide is in, limpets wander about scraping the green **algae** off the rocks. Starfish pull open the shells of their shellfish **prey** while predatory dog whelks go one better and simply drill right through their victim's shell. The seashore is also home to animals with very different feeding methods, as you will see.

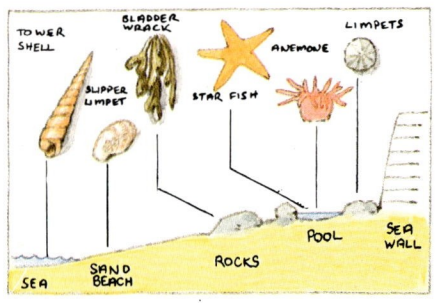

You can make a chart like this, showing the habitat of each specimen you find.

The Seashore Naturalist

To get the best out of your day at the coast, take along some small plastic bottles and boxes for your specimens, a bucket and spade and a wire-mesh sieve for searching for sand-burrowers, and a notebook to keep a record of your finds. If you make a simple sketch of an animal, and notes of where you found it, you can identify it later from a field-guide, either at home or in your local library.

Later, you can make attractive displays of your finds for your room at home or for the school classroom. Or you can use shells of different shapes and colours to make and decorate presents.

Remember that this book is just a starter. There are many more things to discover – whether your main interest turns out to be birds, plants or the hundreds of small animals living on the shore

SAFETY RULES
1 Do not climb on cliffs
2 Do not wander off alone
3 Keep an eye on the tide so you don't get cut off
4 Always make sure an adult or older brother or sister is within sight
5 Put small animals back where you found them. They will die if you try to take them home
6 Take all your litter home
7 Report any broken glass, metal or chemical containers to the police

Sea Cliffs

Cliffs are the 'high-rise flats' of the coast. Seabirds nest here in their millions, safe from attack by ground **predators** such as stoats, foxes and rats. The steep rocky coastlines of Europe and North America provide homes for enormous **colonies** of gulls, gannets, guillemots, puffins and others. The puffins nest in burrows in the cliff-top soil, but most cliff-breeders lay their eggs on tiny ledges on the cliff face.

Hard rocks like granite and limestone give very steep cliffs. The lack of soil means that few plants can find a root-hold, and those that do take root must be able to survive high winds, scorching sun and constant drenching with salt spray. Softer rocks like shales and clays wear away more easily. They produce more sloping cliffs, which support a bigger variety of plants and animals.

HERRING GULL
The most common of the big gulls. Nests on cliffs and sand dunes, often in huge colonies, but is also seen inland in towns. Herring Gulls are powerful fliers, soaring and gliding on the wind. They eat almost anything – preying on shellfish and crabs, and **scavenging** behind fishing boats and on city rubbish tips.
Length: 56–66 cm

DATE _____

PLACE _____

GUILLEMOT

Although not related to the penguins of the southern oceans, guillemots have a similar appearance and lifestyle. They breed in dense cliff-ledge colonies and feed on small fish, which they catch in shallow hunting dives made from the surface while swimming in large groups called 'rafts'.
Length: 40–43 cm

DATE _____

PLACE _____

GANNET

These large handsome seabirds are superb fliers, soaring and wheeling on the air currents around their cliff nest sites. They make spectacular dives from 30 metres or more when hunting, and enter the water with their metre-long wings folded back in arrow formation.
Length: 85–100 cm

DATE _____

PLACE _____

THRIFT
Also called the Sea Pink. Grows on cliffs and in salt marshes, and is also found on mountains inland. The dense cushion of leaves forms a tight clump close to the ground – the best protection against strong winds which might easily uproot a tall plant. Flowers between April and August.
Height: about 15 cm

DATE _____

PLACE _____

SEA BUCKTHORN
A thorny shrub which grows well on cliffs and dunes, and is also found inland on the banks of mountain streams. The tiny green flowers open between March and April and in winter the bright orange berries provide a source of food for birds.
Height: up to 3 metres

DATE _____

PLACE _____

SEA MAYWEED

The Mayweed is a member of the daisy family, found on cliffs and dunes and fields near the sea. Its flowers have a yellow centre surrounded by white petals, and the leaves are narrow and fleshy, branching into numerous feathery leaflets. The plant grows upright in sheltered places but often the stems grow along the ground.
Height: up to 70 cm

DATE _____

PLACE _____

WILD CARROT

The Wild Carrot is a tall hairy **herb** which grows on cliffs and dunes and in dry grassy areas. It has a tough stem with vertical ridges, and feathery leaves. The large flat-topped flowerhead is made up of numerous separate flowers, mostly white but usually with a red or purple one in the middle.
Height: 25–100 cm

DATE _____

PLACE _____

Rock and Shingle Shores

Shingle beaches are harsh places in which to try to make a living. The loose stones are constantly in motion, rolled about by every tide and storm wave so that small animals would soon be crushed and even the toughest seaweeds find it impossible to hold on.

Rocky shores, on the other hand, are often teeming with life. This is still a tough place to live – pounded by the waves and alternately covered by the incoming tide then left high and dry as the tide goes out again. But animal life has become adapted to cope with these conditions. Seaweeds have tough anchors and flexible fronds that sway with the waves, and many animals have thick shells to protect them, and to hold enough moisture to prevent them drying out between tides. Others keep cool and damp by hiding under seaweed.

ROCK PIPIT
This busy shorebird eats its own weight in food every day. It scurries about, taking small periwinkles from the rocks and picking the **larvae** of sandflies and midges from amongst the piles of rotting seaweed. Its simple grassy nest is tucked away in a rock crevice for protection.
Length: 16–17 cm

DATE _____

PLACE _____

TURNSTONE

Turnstones visit the shores of Europe twice a year as they travel between their Arctic breeding grounds and their African summer quarters. The name comes from their distinctive habit of turning over seaweeds and stones to get at the sand-hoppers, worms and small molluscs hiding underneath.
Length: 23 cm

DATE _____

PLACE _____

OYSTERCATCHER

Unmistakable in its smart black and white plumage and brilliant orange bill – specially adapted for opening the cockles and mussels that are its main food. Roosting birds often gather in large flocks and stand together on the shore, all facing the same way.
Length: 42–44 cm

DATE _____

PLACE _____

YELLOW HORNED POPPY
A common seaside flower on shingle and coarse sand. The leaves and stems are bluish-green and ooze a sticky yellow liquid when broken. The deep yellow flowers appear from June to September but the plant's most distinctive feature is the long green pod (up to 30 cm) holding the seeds.
Height: 25–90 cm

DATE _____

PLACE _____

SEA CAMPION
Common on rocks and shingle and also found on gravel banks of mountain streams. The plant is a **perennial** (one that flowers year after year) and its tough, woody stems spread out along the ground before sending up their blue-green flowering shoots and leaves.
Height: up to 25 cm

DATE _____

PLACE _____

SEA-KALE

A perennial member of the cabbage family, with small white, sweet-smelling flowers which appear between June and August. The lower leaves are large, thick and deeply lobed along the edges, but the younger upper leaves are smooth and narrow. The young growing shoots can be eaten as a vegetable.
Height: 40–60 cm

DATE _____

PLACE _____

SHEEP'S BIT

A tall hairy herb found on cliffs and shingle beaches and in dry areas inland. The tall, straight, flowering stems branch near the base and are free of leaves except near the bottom where there are short fleshy leaves with toothed edges.
Height: up to 50 cm

DATE _____

PLACE _____

Seaweeds

Seaweeds are the main plant life around the shores of the world's oceans. When the tide is out they sag and sprawl over rocks and breakwaters, often rather unattractive with their smooth, slightly slimy surface and strong smell. But look again as the tide comes in. Once the seaweeds are supported by the water their real beauty can be seen. Some have strap-like fronds many metres long. Others are delicate and feathery. Some have air bladders to help them float, while others have tough, many-branched anchors called 'holdfasts' to resist the surge of storm waves.

There are three main types. Green seaweeds grow in shallow water close to shore. Brown seaweeds range from the beach down into deep water. And weeds of the smaller red group grow at depths of 100 metres and more.

SEA LETTUCE
Sea lettuce fronds are broad, pale green and almost transparent. They grow on rocks from the upper shore to below low water, and also in rock pools. The fronds can be any shape but are always broader at the top than at the stalk. Broken fronds are sometimes washed up on the beach.
Length: up to 50 cm

DATE _____

PLACE _____

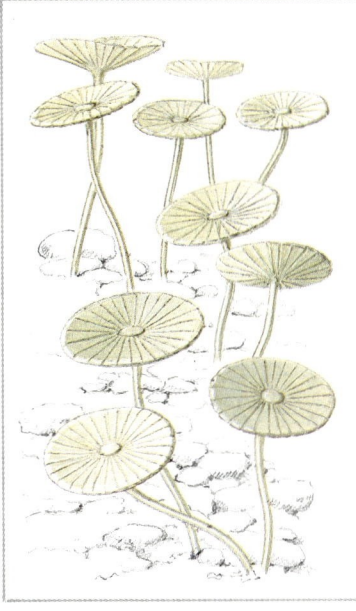

MERMAID'S CUP
This delicate umbrella-shaped seaweed is found on rocks and in rock pools around the Mediterranean. The flat disc at the top of the stiff stalk is not solid but is made up of up to 100 segments, rather like the petals of a daisy.
Height: up to 8 cm

DATE _____

PLACE _____

FROND WEED
This dark green weed forms dense mats on the middle and lower shore. It often grows amongst the longer brown seaweeds like Toothed Wrack and Bladder Wrack. Full-grown plants send out runners which then develop into new clumps of weed, so the Frond Weed can quickly spread over large areas.
Length: up to 12 cm

DATE _____

PLACE _____

KNOTTED WRACK

The tough leathery fronds of Knotted Wrack get their name from the large air bladders spaced every few centimetres along the rounded stem. The weed grows on rocky Atlantic, English Channel and North Sea shores. Sometimes it has tufts of the red weed, Polysiphonia, growing on it.
Length: 25–150 cm

DATE _____

PLACE _____

BLADDER WRACK

Fronds are broader and flatter than those of the Knotted Wrack. Another distinctive feature is the rib along the middle of the frond. The air bladders are in clusters of two or three. Bladder Wrack often forms a distinctive zone between high and low water marks on the shoreline.
Length: 15–100 cm

DATE _____

PLACE _____

OARWEED

A thick, heavy seaweed with leathery strap-like fronds branching from the top of a thick round stalk. The holdfast has a large number of branches, like the roots of a tree. Oarweed grows on rocks right at the water's edge and down to about five metres below water. Pieces of the fronds are often washed up on the beach.
Length: up to 2 metres

DATE _____

PLACE _____

SEA BELT

The broad blade of the Sea Belt is three or four times as long as its thin stalk, and has a characteristic wrinkled appearance. The holdfast has many branches. Sea Belt grows on rocks at the water's edge and down to depths of 20 metres or more in sheltered bays.
Length: up to 3 metres

DATE _____

PLACE _____

SAND-HOPPER
Very common among stones, seaweed and rubbish washed up on the beach. The head has two sets of **antennae** – the upper ones short, the lower ones much longer. The second legs have tiny pincers, the third pair have large ones that are quite easy to see. Hoppers jump about when they are disturbed.
Length: 1–2 cm

DATE _____

PLACE _____

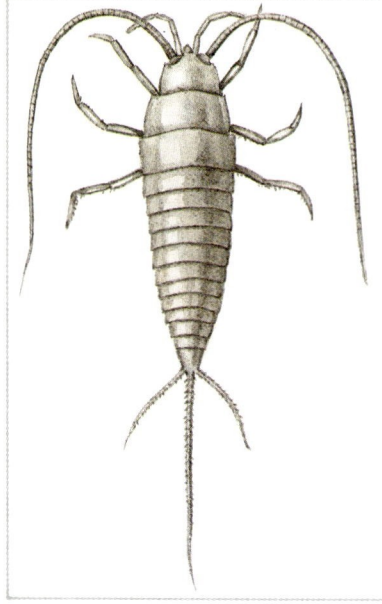

BRISTLETAIL
One of the few insects specialized for shore life. The thin segmented body has three pairs of walking legs but no wings. The antennae on the head, and the slender bristle-like 'tail', are both almost as long as the insect's body. Bristletails live in cracks in the rocks and between stones.
Length: about 1 cm

DATE _____

PLACE _____

COAT-OF-MAIL CHITON
Chitons are small members of the **mollusc** family. The upper side of the body is covered by eight shell plates and the animal clings to the rocks with a muscular foot, rather like a snail. Chitons are found on rocks and clinging to shells on the shore and in shallow water.
Length: 1–2 cm

DATE _____

PLACE _____

SEA SPIDER
The long-legged sea spider inhabits shallow waters and rock pools near the water's edge, often among seaweeds and barnacles. The body is long and thin and is held high when the spider walks about. As well as four pairs of walking legs, the spider has pincer-like feeding claws near the head.
Length: body 1 cm, legs 2½ cm

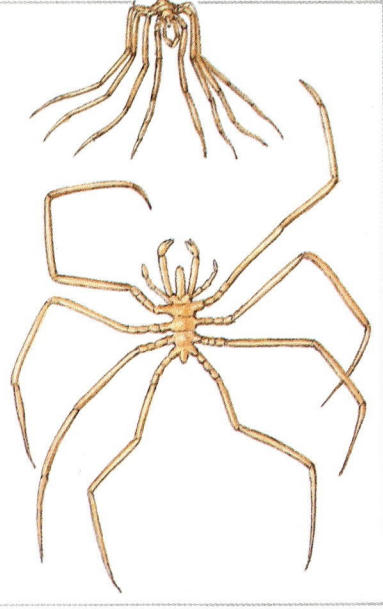

DATE _____

PLACE _____

Rock Pools

Of all the different types of shore, rock pools are probably the best hunting grounds for naturalists. They are like small natural **aquariums**, full of life, all within easy reach without any need for special equipment. To get the most out of a rock pool, try to study it at different times of the day – just before the tide comes in, when the sea is washing into the pool, and again when the tide is well out. That way you will begin to discover how the inhabitants live. Many of them hide when the tide is out, safe from attack by seabirds and to avoid being dried out by the sun and wind. But once the sea washes in, carrying food for many of them, limpets start to wander over the rocks, colourful sea anemones put out their tentacles, starfish go out hunting, crabs scuttle about and all manner of activity is there for you to watch.

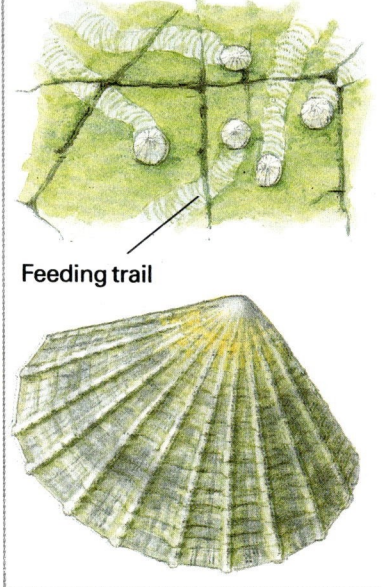

Feeding trail

COMMON LIMPET
Limpets are found all over the exposed rocks of the shore. When the tide is in, they move about – scraping algae off the rocks with a rasp-like tongue. But when the tide is out (or if you touch one) the animal clamps its shell tight against the rock – fitting neatly into a groove worn by the sharp edge of the shell.
Length: up to 7 cm

DATE _____

PLACE _____

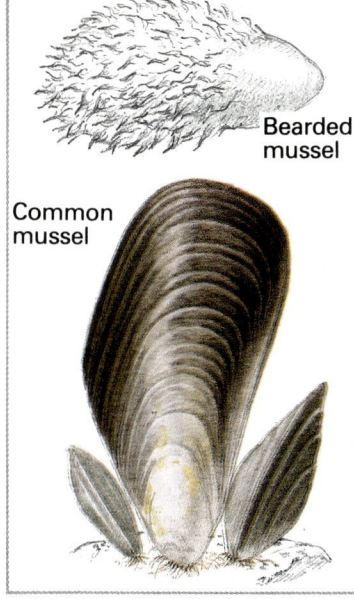

Bearded mussel

Common mussel

COMMON MUSSEL
Clusters of dark blue-black mussels are a familiar sight on rocks low down on the shore. They are often found along with barnacles and other animals. Note the tough threads that anchor the shell to the rock. Look out also for the smaller Bearded Horse Mussel with its coat of coarse whiskers.
Length: up to 10 cm

DATE _____

PLACE _____

ACORN BARNACLE
Barnacles are a fascinating example of nature's **marine** engineering. The conical shell has a central diamond-shaped opening protected by movable plates of shell. When covered by the sea, the animal opens this 'hatch' and extends its feeding tentacles to sweep tiny food particles from the water.
Length: up to 1½ cm

DATE _____

PLACE _____

DOG WHELK
Dog Whelk shells are grey or cream in colour, often with brown spiral markings. They are common on rocky shores and in pools, and are often found amongst barnacles and mussels, on which they are predators. The whelk may not look like a killer but it can rasp a hole right through the shell of a barnacle to feed on the animal inside.
Height: about 3 cm

DATE _____

PLACE _____

COMMON STARFISH
The brownish-yellow Common Starfish has plump tapering arms covered with small blunt spines. The undersides have large numbers of tiny tube-feet ending in suckers which are used for moving about and for pulling open the shellfish on which it feeds. These starfish are found in rock pools and on stony seabeds down to 200 metres.

Diameter: 6–12 cm (deep water specimens up to 50 cm)

DATE _____

PLACE _____

BRITTLESTAR

The delicate red, orange, brown or purple brittlestar may be found under stones and weeds in rock pools and down to 300 metres. The body is round or five-sided, with five bands of spines running from the centre. The arms are covered with fine spines. They are easily damaged, but are quickly regrown if broken.
Diameter (body): up to 2 cm

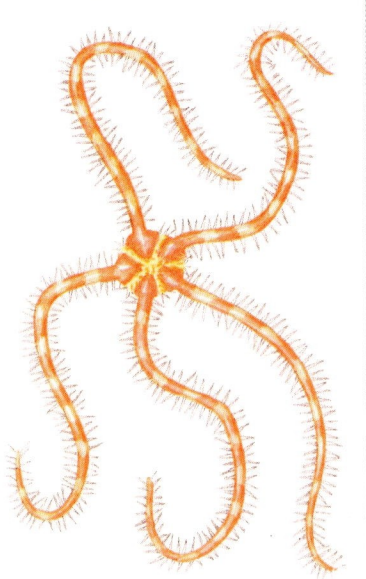

DATE _____

PLACE _____

EDIBLE SEA URCHIN

Empty sea urchin shells are sometimes found in rock pools, and are often sold as seaside souvenirs. In life, the shell is covered with short thick spines, and long tube feet protrude from the rows of small holes that radiate from the middle of the shell.
Diameter: up to 12 cm

Empty shell

DATE _____

PLACE _____

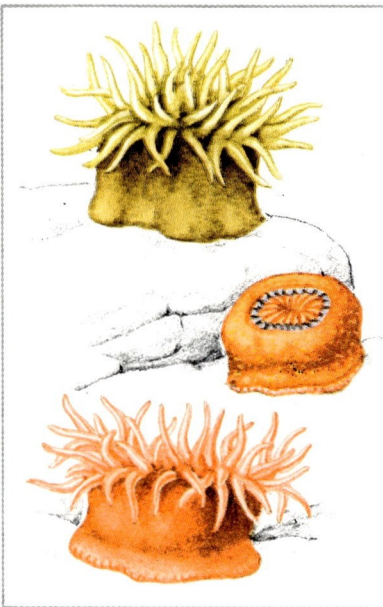

BEADLET ANEMONE
Beadlet Anemones may be red, green, brown or even red with green spots (the 'strawberry' variety). The smooth body is up to 7 cm tall and is topped by about 200 small feeding tentacles in six circles. The tentacles are pulled inside the body when the tide goes out or if the animal is threatened. Lives in rock pools and down to 8 metres.
Diameter: up to 6 cm

DATE _____

PLACE _____

SNAKELOCK ANEMONE
Found in pools and down to 20 metres in clear waters. Body is larger than that of the Beadlet, but flatter and bag-like. Tentacles are up to 15 cm long and cannot be completely pulled in. A white line runs from either side of the mouth to the ring of tentacles.
Diameter: up to 15 cm

DATE _____

PLACE _____

CHAMELEON PRAWN

The prawn gets its name from its ability to change colour to match its background. It is green, brown or red by day, swimming among rocks and seaweeds in rock pools and coastal waters. At night the prawn is a transparent blue. The main antennae are about half the body-length.
Length: up to 2½ cm

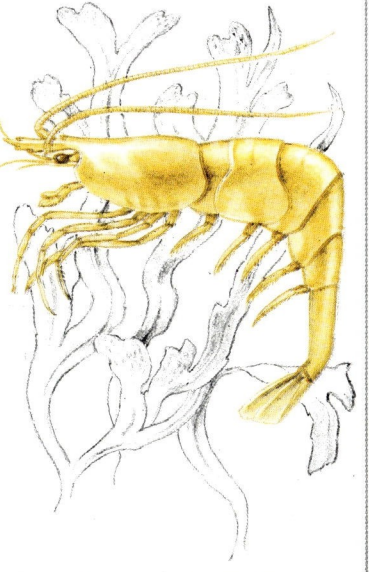

DATE _____

PLACE _____

COMMON LOBSTER

Lives in caves below water and in holes between rocks and under seaweed. The body is dark blue-black with red antennae. The first pair of walking legs have huge pincers that can be quite dangerous. The tough plates covering the body are sometimes washed up on the beach.
Length: up to 50 cm

DATE _____

PLACE _____

SPIDER CRAB
Unmistakable pear-shaped body with two long pointed projections between the eyes. The upper side of the shell has seven thorny spikes and is usually covered with seaweeds and small animals like sponges and marine worms. The crab usually hides among seaweeds.
Length (shell): up to 2 cm

DATE _____

PLACE _____

EDIBLE CRAB
The Edible Crab has a very distinctive oval shell with a crinkled edge like a pie-crust. The shell is orange-pink to brown, with black tips to the large pincers. The crab lives among rocks low down on the shore. Very large specimens are sometimes caught in deep water.
Width of shell: up to 25 cm

DATE _____

PLACE _____

COMMON SHORE CRAB

Very common crab on both sandy and rocky shores. The shell varies from dark green to brown above, and is paler yellow-green beneath. The front edge of the shell has five sharp teeth (like a saw) at either side of the small black eyes. The front legs carry heavy pincers.
Width of shell: up to 10 cm

DATE _____

PLACE _____

VELVET SWIMMING CRAB

Lives amongst stones in pools and down to about ten metres in the sea. Body is dark brown and covered with fine hairs. The eyes are bright red, and there are blue bands around the legs. The rear legs are flattened into paddles for swimming.
Width of shell: up to 12 cm

Swimming 'paddle'

DATE _____

PLACE _____

CONGER EEL
A powerful thick-bodied predator, with a slightly jutting upper jaw. Feeds mainly on octopus and crabs. The body is smooth, without scales, and is dark brown above and cream below. Found in both shallow and deep waters, in caves, wrecks and holes among rocks.
Length: up to 2 metres

DATE _____

PLACE _____

FIFTEEN-SPINED STICKLEBACK
This slender-bodied sea fish has a long tapering head and a jutting lower jaw. It feeds mainly on small **crustaceans** among seaweeds and rocks. The fish lives in pools and stony estuaries, and in shallow coastal waters.
Length: up to 20 cm

DATE _____

PLACE _____

SEAHORSE

A very unusual inhabitant of seaweed and seagrass beds from the Mediterranean as far north as the approaches to the English Channel. The animal spends most of its time anchored by the tail to a piece of weed, reaching out with its long snout to pick off floating morsels of **plankton** food.
Length: up to 15 cm

DATE _____

PLACE _____

CORKWING WRASSE

A common fish of rock pools and shallow-water seaweed beds from the Mediterranean north to the North Sea and Baltic Sea. More colourful than many inshore fishes. The dark spot near the tail is a good identification mark for this species.
Length: up to 20 cm

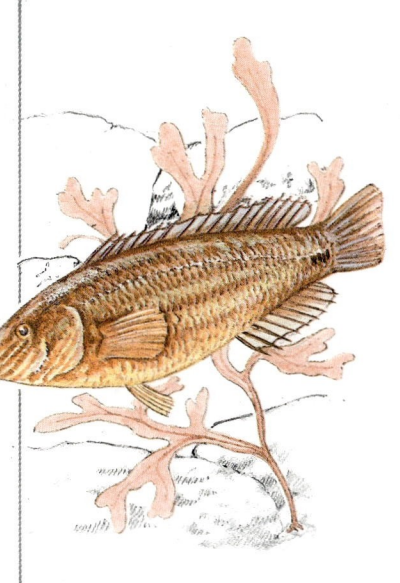

DATE _____

PLACE _____

Sandy Shorelines

The pounding waves that break pieces of rock from a cliff face do not stop there. The rock fragments are thrown against other rocks and broken into smaller and smaller pieces. They may end up as part of a shingle beach, rolled against other pebbles until they are smooth and round. Or they may continue to break up, until what was once a lump of granite, or sandstone or limestone is reduced to tiny shimmering grains of quartz and other minerals. Where there are shellfish beds or reefs close to shore, beaches may consist entirely of powdered shell and coral.

Sand is constantly on the move – carried along the coast by waves and currents, and piled up behind the beach by the wind. At first glance, sand dunes and beaches look barren and deserted, but under the surface they too are full of life.

RINGED PLOVER
The distinctive head and breast markings and bold wing-bars make the Ringed Plover an easy bird to identify. Flocks feed on sandy shores and mud flats, alternately running then pausing, and often stirring up worms and other sand-dwellers with a characteristic paddling movement of one foot.
Length: 19 cm

DATE _____

PLACE _____

SANDERLING
Sanderlings are mainly summer and winter visitors to Europe's shores, but some stay all year. They feed on beaches in small flocks, dashing about like clockwork toys as they feed up for their long migrations from the Arctic to as far south as South Africa, Australia and the Falkland Islands.
Length: 18–20 cm

DATE _____

PLACE _____

KNOT
One of the largest of the European shore feeders. Also distinctive because of its dramatic change from grey-white winter plumage to rich red-brown breeding plumage in summer. Knot feed in large flocks. The birds move forward, then pause to probe the sand three or four times.
Length: about 25 cm

DATE _____

PLACE _____

Marram   Couch

MARRAM AND SAND COUCH

Marram and Sand Couch are both perennial grasses that spread by sending out long underground stems. These act as a food store through the winter. Marram grass is very tough and is often planted to stabilize shifting dunes. Sand Couch is usually found on new dunes.
Height: Marram 50–125 cm
Couch 25–60 cm

DATE _____

PLACE _____

SEA SANDWORT

A yellow-green perennial herb with plump leaves growing in pairs along thick stems. The flowers are small and greenish-white. Sea Sandwort roots easily in sand, and is a common plant on dunes and on the upper parts of sand and shingle beaches.
Height: up to 25 cm

DATE _____

PLACE _____

SEA BINDWEED

Sea Bindweed is one of the most attractive plants of sand and shingle. It has rich green kidney-shaped leaves, and delicate pink or pale purple flowers. Sea Bindweed creeps along the ground, unlike its larger relative the Hedge Bindweed which climbs by twining around other plants.
Height: about 5 cm

DATE _____

PLACE _____

SEA HOLLY

A medium-sized plant of sand and shingle shores. The upright stem is topped by a flowerhead of tiny pale blue flowers, and the blue-green stem and sharply spiked blue-green leaves are veined with white and covered with a 'bloom'. The fruits are covered with tiny hooks.
Height: 10–60 cm

DATE _____

PLACE _____

The Seashore Burrowers

The reason why sandy shores appear at first sight to have no life is that most of the animals are burrowers. The constantly moving surface offers no firm foundation for the anemones, snails and other fixed animals of rocky shores. And to remain on the smooth flat surface after the tide has gone out would make any animal a sitting target for the hungry seabirds that patrol overhead. So – the only safe place at low tide is down beneath the sand.

Look at the damp surface at low tide. Everywhere there are small conical pits, and near each one a mound of sand, coiled in loops like an old bootlace. These mark the ends of lugworm burrows. Elsewhere you may spot the feeding tubes of buried cockles, or sea urchins, the cemented tubes of sand masons or the projecting tips of buried razor shells.

MASKED CRAB
The shell, or **carapace**, of the Masked Crab is long and narrow, with one small spine and one large one at each side. The long hairy antennae lie side by side, and form a tube to the surface when the crab is buried in the sand. The male crab's front legs are twice the length of the carapace. Those of the female are much shorter.
Length (shell): up to 4 cm

DATE _____

PLACE _____

LUGWORM
Very common sand worm that lives in a U-shaped burrow. It feeds on tiny particles of food in the sand, which it passes through its body leaving the tell-tale **casts** on the surface. The body is thick and rounded, and tapers to the tail. Each body segment from 7 to 20 carries a pair of bright red, feathery gills.
Length: up to 20 cm

DATE _____

PLACE _____

SAND MASON
Look out for the masons' tubes sticking out of the sand on the lower shore and in shallow water. They are made of sand grains and shell fragments cemented together. The worm lives permanently in its tube. The thicker front part of the body has three pairs of tufted red gills and a mass of pale yellow pink feeding tentacles.
Length: up to 30 cm

DATE _____

PLACE _____

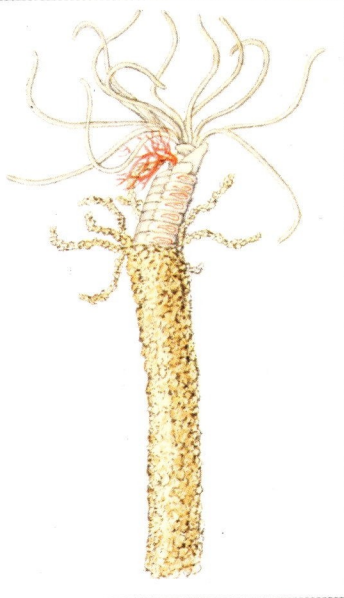

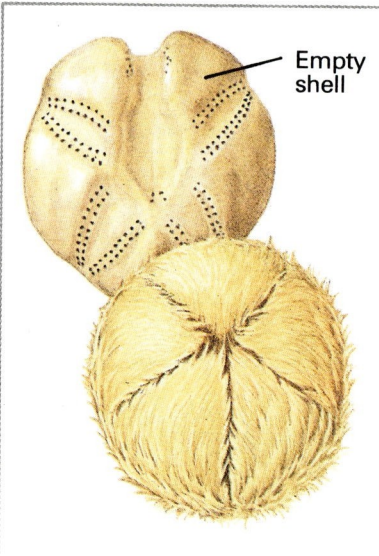

Empty shell

HEART URCHIN
This small burrowing sea urchin is also called the Sea Potato. It is a pale yellow-brown and covered with short dense backward-sloping spines which give it an almost furry look. Lives on the lower shore and down to 200 metres. Look out also for the larger violet-coloured Purple Heart Urchin in coarse sand and gravel.
Length: up to 9 cm

DATE _____

PLACE _____

COMMON COCKLE
A thick, heavily-ridged oval shell in which the two parts, called **valves**, are almost identical. Look at the interlocking teeth and grooves that make up the hinge, and also the smooth areas inside the shell where the muscles were attached for opening and closing the shell.
Length: up to 5 cm

Hinge

DATE _____

PLACE _____

THIN TELLIN
Often called the 'Butterfly Shell' because the valves are frequently found still joined by the tough hinge ligament. The valves are smooth and delicate, and every shade of red, pink, orange and yellow, both inside and out. Tellins live in the sand and feed through long tubes (siphons) extended to the surface.
Length: up to 2 cm

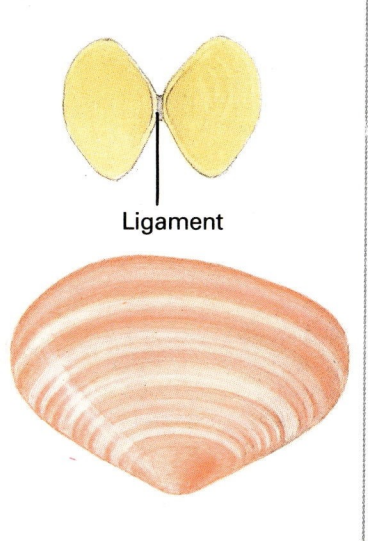
Ligament

DATE _____

PLACE _____

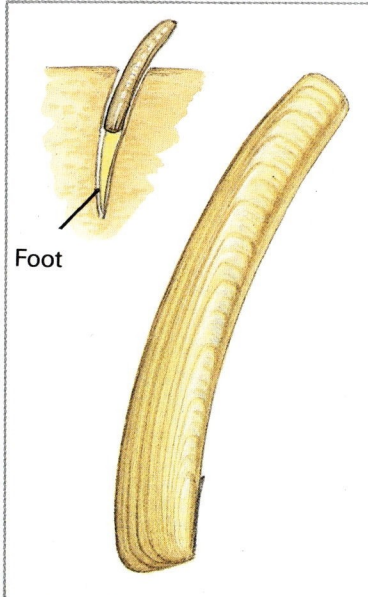
Foot

RAZOR SHELL
Razor shells are long two-valved shells that 'stand' upright in the sand with the top of the shell above the surface. When the tide goes out, or if danger threatens, the animal can pull itself quickly into the sand using a powerful muscular foot that protrudes from the lower end of the shell.
Length: up to 12 cm

DATE _____

PLACE _____

LESSER SAND EEL
A slender-bodied fish with a pointed head and jutting lower jaw. Common in areas of fine clean sand. Eels swim in large groups and often burrow into the sand. They are an important source of food for herrings and mackerel, and also for terns, puffins and other seabirds.
Length: Up to 20 cm

DATE _____

PLACE _____

WEEVER FISH
Stay clear of this one! The Weever lives in shallow sandy-bottomed waters in the Mediterranean, Atlantic, English Channel and North Sea. It often lies buried in the sand, and the danger lies in the poisoned spines on the long **dorsal** fin and on the edge of the gill covers.
Length: up to 35 cm

DATE _____

PLACE _____

SAND GOBY
A small fish, beautifully camouflaged for life on a sandy sea-bed. Like most sea-bed fish, the eyes are on top of the head and the mouth is designed to grab prey swimming overhead. The male has a blue spot on the first dorsal fin, and all Sand Gobies have bands of darker-coloured scales down their sides.
Length: up to 9 cm

DATE _____

PLACE _____

FLOUNDER
Like sole, turbot and plaice, the flounder is completely adapted to life on the sea bed. The fish lies on its side with its green-brown upper side perfectly camouflaged against sand, gravel or mud in coastal waters and estuaries. Both eyes are positioned on the uppermost side of the head.
Length: up to 20 cm

DATE _____

PLACE _____

Exploring the Strand Line

As a change from looking at the animals and plants of cliffs, rock pools and beaches, try the gentle art of beachcombing. Along the upper part of the beach, at the point reached by the high tide, you will find a band of dead seaweed and other bits and pieces thrown up by the waves. This jumble of natural and man-made debris can prove an interesting place to search. In addition to its own collection of small animals it is often visited by birds looking for a quick snack, but along the strand line you will also find cuttlefish bones, dogfish egg cases, pieces of wood with holes bored by piddocks and ship worms. You may come across shells of shore-nesting birds and the bleached skulls and bones of seabirds, or perhaps deep-water shells thrown onto the beach by waves. And finally, there are man-made objects like fishing floats.

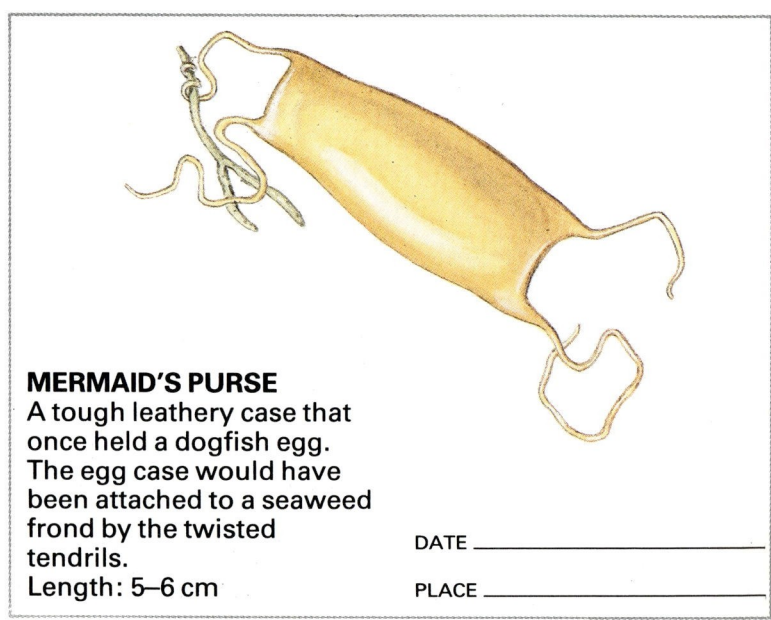

MERMAID'S PURSE
A tough leathery case that once held a dogfish egg. The egg case would have been attached to a seaweed frond by the twisted tendrils.
Length: 5–6 cm

DATE _____

PLACE _____

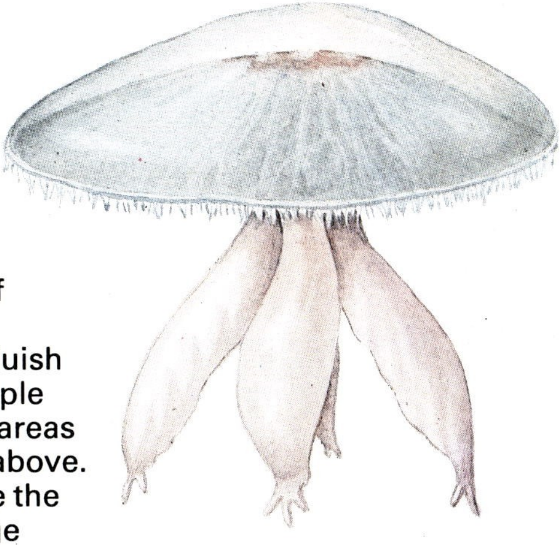

MOON JELLY
Common jellyfish of European shores. Transparent, pale bluish colour with four purple horse-shoe shaped areas when viewed from above. Tiny tentacles fringe the 'umbrella': four large feeding tentacles hang beneath.
Diameter: up to 20 cm

DATE _____

PLACE _____

Ship worm tube

SHIP WORM
A shellfish that looks like a worm. The animal is long and thin and the shell valves form a horny cap at the head, used for drilling through the wood of boats and pier supports. As the animal bores a hole, its body makes a lining substance that is often left as a hard white tube.
Tube length: up to 20 cm

DATE _____

PLACE _____

CUTTLEBONE
The lightweight oval bone that forms the skeleton of a cuttlefish.
Length: up to 16 cm

DATE _____

PLACE _____

VARIEGATED SCALLOP
An attractive ridged shell with unequal 'wings' at either side of the hinge. Lives either attached to the sea-bed or swimming free.
Length: up to 6 cm

DATE _____

PLACE _____

Gape

PIDDOCK (above)
The Piddock has an unusual shell with a permanently open gape. One end of the shell is covered with rough tooth-like ribs which help the animal drill through sand, wood and soft rock.
Length: up to 14 cm

DATE _____

PLACE _____

TOWER SHELL (below)
Long slender spiral shells of animals that live half buried in sand or mud on the sea-bed at depths of up to 80 metres offshore.
Length: 3–6 cm

DATE _____

PLACE _____

The Ever-changing Shoreline

Nothing stays the same for very long in the world of nature. Animals and plants grow and die, to be replaced by new generations. And over millions of years entire species come and go, from tiny insects and plants to dinosaurs, elephants and whales. The same is true of the land itself. Whole mountain ranges rise miles into the sky, only to be worn away by rivers and glaciers, wind and rain. And nowhere is the battle more fierce than at the coast, where waves constantly batter the edge of the land and currents carry huge quantities of sand, gravel and mud from one place to another.

The landscape around us is full of clues, and by reading them we can discover what the coastline used to look like, what is happening to it now, and what it may look like in years to come.

One of the golden rules of nature study is to look, and enjoy, and learn without doing any damage. So when you are exploring rock pools or discovering the creatures of the sand or strand line, tread carefully. Replace clumps of seaweed after you have looked underneath, because any small animal that is left uncovered for long is likely to end up as a tasty morsel in the bill of a seabird. There is no harm in picking up a crab for a closer look, but handle it gently, holding it from behind with your thumb on top and fingers underneath out of reach of its pincers, and put it back where you found it after a few minutes.

Building up a collection can be great fun, and it need not cause any damage because most of the objects you will want to keep will be shells, carapaces of crabs that have been shed as the animals grew, and the shell-like cases of sea urchins. Plants too can be collected and dried or pressed, but only take your specimen from a place where there are plenty of plants of that type, and never dig up the entire plant.

Index

Acorn Barnacle 25
Algae 8, 24

Beadlet Anemone 28
Bladder Wrack 19, 20
Bristletail 22
Brittlestar 27

Chameleon Prawn 29
Coat-of-mail Chiton 23
Cockle 40
Conger Eel 32
Corkwing Wrasse 33
Crabs 30–31, 38
Cuttlebone 46
Cuttlefish 44, 46

Dogfish 44
Dog Whelk 26

Edible Sea Urchin 27

Fifteen-spined Stickleback 32
Flounder 3, 43
Frond Weed 19

Gannet 3, 10, 11
Guillemot 10, 11

Heart Urchin 40
Hedge Bindweed 37
Herring Gull 10

Knot 35
Knotted Wrack 20

Lesser Sand Eel 42
Limpet 24
Lobster 29
Lugworm 38, 39

Marram 36
Mermaid's Cup 19
Mermaid's Purse 44
Moon Jelly 45
Mussels 25

Oarweed 21
Oystercatcher 15

Periwinkles 14
Piddock 46
Puffin 3, 10
Purple Heart Urchin 40

Razor Shell 38, 41
Ringed Plover 34
Rock Pipit 14

Sand Couch 36
Sanderling 35
Sand Goby 43
Sand-hopper 15, 22
Sand Mason 38, 39
Sea Belt 21
Sea Bindweed 37
Sea Buckthorn 12
Sea Campion 16
Sea Holly 37
Seahorse 33
Sea-Kale 17
Sea Lettuce 18
Sea Mayweed 13
Sea Sandwort 36
Sea Spider 23
Sheep's Bit 17
Ship Worm 44, 45
Snakelock Anemone 28
Starfish 8, 24, 26

Thin Tellin 41
Thrift 12
Toothed Wrack 19
Tower Shell 46
Turnstone 15

Variegated Scallop 45

Weever Fish 42
Whelk 8
Wild Carrot 13

Yellow Horned Poppy 16